AF879690

How To Break That Curse

All you need to know about curses, how they come into our lives, how they affect us and how to effectively stop them.

First Edition

September 2024

Fr. Stephen Kakande C.S.Sp

Copyright:
Padre Stephen Kakande CSSp.
St. Joseph Parish,
P.O. Box 493,
15 Calle Soledad,
Luquillo, PR 00773
Phone +1-939-425-1970
Email: writetokakande@gmail.com
Website: http://www.stephenkakandecssp.org
www.amazon.com/author/fatherkakandecssp

This book was first published in English by the same author in 2018.
First edition in Spanish 2024.
Published and printed in USA
It is available on Amazon and the Kindle Store.
To access them on Amazon use the following link
www.amazon.com/author/fatherkakandecssp

To pay for your purchase through ATH Móvil use this number +1-939-425-1970

Preface

A curse is an expressed wish or invocation for harm, misfortune, or adversity to befall someone, a place, or an object. It can take various forms, including prayers, imprecations or profane oaths. Throughout history of human existence on earth, curses, whether spoken or believed, have carried significant weight and played a major role in shaping lives of various societies, cultures and religions. The belief in curses has persisted right from the Old Testament times, through ancient Egyptian curses inscribed on tombs, to today's superstitions about the "evil eye", "Santería" and "voodoo".

In today's secularized world, a curse is something that is often disregarded especially with the increased dependence on modern technology. There are people who strongly believe that curses do not exist. Such people argue that what we call curses are nothing but just negative thoughts and behaviours that any human being is capable of. With such an argument, they potentially discredit anything supernatural.

On the other hand, there are people who strongly believe in the existence of curses and their supernatural effects on human beings and the rest of creation. With such a staunch belief, they essentially give credit to the supernatural. For example, some people might believe that a curse is on a particular house, and therefore bringing misfortune to whoever lives in that house. Others might believe that a curse is on a particular spot on the road, thereby causing continued motor accidents and deaths in that same spot. Other people always utter angry curses or profane language against others in frustration or anger. Sometimes misfortune seems to continuously follow some individuals as if in response to an imprecation. A cause of great harm or torment in a life of someone can also be considered a curse. Some people might believe that someone is under a curse if he or she attempts several marriages but without succeeding in any. There are also so many people who are indifferent about the existence of curses. Whatever position you may have on curses, this book will help you acquire immediate understanding of the concept "curse". It contains relevant explanation and references from the scriptures plus testimonies from experienced people. It is with no doubt a useful book to accompany anyone on the journey of faith.

Fr. Stephen Kakande Sekayala C.S.Sp

Table of Contents

Introduction

It was a Tuesday morning, shortly before mid-day. A young lady came to the parish office and requested to see me. Her belly had expanded and protruded out, above the size that is generally considered normal. It was probably a few inches perpendicular of her chin. A sign that she was pregnant -- about five months pregnancy. Physically, she externally looked much younger and very attractive so much that if your yardstick is someone's facial looks alone then you would place her in an age category where she did not belong. On the contrary, she was in her mid-thirties, yet had a teenage face with looks of innocence beyond age and comparison. She approached me and then spoke to me with a smile on her face. She said,

> ***"Since the day you prayed with us at home, my relationship with my mother improved. She accepted me to continue living with my husband. She even accepted me to come back and live with him in our house. Now we live together with her and my husband in the same house without any problem which was impossible in the past eight years. I conceived after eight years of struggle—moving from doctor to doctor in search for medical solution which was never acquired. Now I am five months pregnant. I thank God that I conceived three weeks after you prayed with us at our home. Indeed, prayers work. Bro Stephen, I want***

to thank you. You have opened my eyes to Jesus. Because of you I have asked Jesus, to empty me of me and fill me of Him. I am glad that I have found someone to show me how to love Jesus"...

The above happened in Trinidad and Tobago. I met that young lady in Arouca, a town located in the stretch towards the Eastern part of Trinidad Island. She was in a serious problematic situation after her mother had disowned her and pronounced cursing words against her, for being in a love affair with a boyfriend of a race which is different from hers. Apart from a multiplicity of problems that surrounded her, she failed to conceive even when all possible solutions had been sought from the medical science arena. After careful spiritual discernment, I realised that there was a sort of a curse operating in her life. That curse always kept her in the bondage of barrenness. I asked her to organise herself and meet as a family in prayer to break that curse. She did as I requested her. I mediated the reconciliation process between her and her mother and we prayed for the breaking of any curse that could be lingering in her life. It is after breaking this curse through prayer that she was able to conceive and later gave birth to a child.

Perhaps you may know someone whose pattern of life is in a total mess. You are wondering why it is so. Probably it is you yourself wondering why you cannot have a serious breakthrough in spite of your effort and commitment. The answer is: there might be a curse operating against you in order to keep you in bondage. And without breaking this curse you might never have a serious breakthrough.

What is a Curse

According to www.bing.com , a curse is defined as “a solemn utterance intended to invoke a supernatural power to inflict harm or punishment on someone or something”. Related to this, Merriam-Webster dictionary defines curse as “a prayer or invocation for harm or injury to come upon someone”. In both definitions the words that stand out clearly demonstrate the characteristics of a curse. These include:

1. Utterance—meaning that a curse is a spoken word pronounced by one’s mouth.
2. Supernatural—a curse is charged by supernatural power.
3. Harm—a curse is harmful. It generates disastrous and unpleasant situations to its victims.
4. Punishment—a curse is a form of punishment to an individual or group or a nation.
5. Invocation—a curse does not just happen anyhow. It is always something that is invoked.

6. Prayer—a curse takes up a form of negative prayer. A prayer can actually curse.

Forms of Curses

Curses come in many forms but the damage they cause is the same. There are three major forms of curses. These include:

1. Generational curse
2. Family controlling curse and
3. Personal / self-imposed curse

1. Generational Curse

A generational curse is the one that manifests itself in the lives of individuals or groups of individuals or nations stemming from the past ancestors through the present to the future generations. It refers to patterns of negative consequences that seem to affect multiple generations within a family. It is the commonest form of a curse that haunts many people even though it is regarded least by many.

The root of generational sin goes back to the fall of humanity. When Adam and Eve sinned in the Garden of Eden as seen in Genesis chapters 1 and 2, their disobedience introduced sin into the world. As a result, all of humanity inherited a sinful nature. We are born with a propensity toward sin (Psalm 51:5; Romans 5:12). That does not necessarily mean that a generational curse is a direct curse from God. Instead, it involves the passing down of certain behaviors, tendencies, or consequences from one generation to the next. Those patterns can affect physical, emotional, and spiritual aspects of a family line from generation to generation.

Generational curses can manifest in different behavioral patterns whereby families may struggle with similar sins or destructive behaviors across generations e.g., addiction, anger, divorce etc. Emotional Wounds as a result of unresolved emotional pain or trauma can be passed down from generation to generation thereby forming a generational curse…

Likewise, generational curses may manifest through Spiritual Bondage and physical health whereby families may face spiritual strongholds or generational ties to false beliefs or idolatry whilst certain health conditions or vulnerabilities may recur. In summary, generational curses are not necessarily God's direct punishment but rather the result of sin's impact on families over time. Children and grandchildren inherit and greatly suffer the consequences of the sins of their parents, grandparents and great grandparents—who were also affected by the sins of their ancestors. The ultimate solution to generational curses lies in turning to Jesus, who breaks the chains of sin and offers freedom to all generations, both present and the past.

2. Family Controlling Curse

This is a form of a curse whose consequences manifests in almost all members of the same family. It refers to patterns of negative influence or behavior that seem to persist in the lives of parents and siblings within the same family. This type of curse involves recurring dynamics, attitudes, or actions that exert control over family members. These patterns can impact various aspects of family life, including relationships, decision-making, and emotional well-being. Families affected by controlling curses often exhibit similar behaviors or responses among all members. Such behaviors may limit individual freedom or autonomy. Family members may feel suffocated or unable to make decisions autonomously or may feel pressured to conform to certain norms or expectations.

How does a Family Controlling Curse Operate?

A curse can follow individuals through their family tree. In a certain family, you may find that an evil pattern follows each and every member hailing from such a family.

Too many recurring problems such as alcoholism, womanizing, divorce, barrenness, financial problems, poverty, polygamy, marriage failures, unexplainable accidents, adultery, incest, satanism, spiritism, sorcery, cohabitation, suicide, sexual perversion etc can all be consequences of a family controlling curse.

There are some family controlling curses that bring about failures and uniformity to every member who is born in such a family. That is why some families are known for evil practices such as sexual promiscuity, womanizing and adultery—every male born in such a family becomes a prolific womanizer; and every woman born in such a family becomes a renowned adulterer who can even leave her own husband in bed at midnight and tip-toe to the neighbourhood for a quick sexual activity even when she is pregnant.

Other families are known for abject poverty; whoever tries to succeed financially in such a family still fails. A certain calamity or loss can befall him or her until he or she falls back to poverty. Other family lineages will always have a deaf and dumb or crippled person in every one of its generations while others will always have a mad person or people with mental disorders.

Other families are known for committing suicide while others are known for wizardly, witchcraft, santeria, obeah and voodoo. Some families are known for incestuous relationships, while others are known for poor academic performance; in a way that every child born in such a family is intellectually dense. All these are curses and bondages that monitor people bringing about failures and poverty among them. It's only through prayers of breaking curses that such families can be redeemed.

3.Personal / Self Imposed Curse

A personal or self-imposed curse is the one that comes into our lives when we choose sin and evil over goodness. It refers to negative consequences or limitations that we bring upon ourselves through our own words, thoughts, or actions. Self-imposed curses arise from our own choices and attitudes. It also sometimes arise from the negative words that we pronounce about ourselves. Such words may include for example 'I am not lucky', 'I am not as blessed as other people', 'I cannot do that' etc...etc... Such words sometimes get charged with negative energies that make a person be exactly what he/she pronounces on him/herself. Our spoken words carry power. When we speak negatively about ourselves or others, we can unintentionally create a curse. For example, saying, "I will never succeed" or "I'm always unlucky" can reinforce negative outcomes. Our internal beliefs too, shape our reality. If we believe we are unworthy, undeserving, or doomed to fail, we may unknowingly curse ourselves by aligning with those beliefs. Repeatedly affirming negative statements about ourselves e.g., “I'm a failure,” “I'll never find love”, “I will never marry” can reinforce those beliefs and hinder progress in the life of an individual. Proverbs 18:21 says, “Death and life are in the power of the tongue.” Our words matter. Romans 12:2 encourages us to renew our minds and not conform to negative patterns. Believing that we are not good enough, smart enough, or deserving enough can hold us back. Also, constantly fearing the worst or expecting disaster can create a self-fulfilling prophecy. Engaging in behaviors that harm our well-being e.g., procrastination, addiction etc… can turn into a form of self-imposed curse.

What Scripture Say About Curses

There is a lot in the bible written concerning curses and of course blessings. Proverbs 3:33 says ***“The Lord's curse is on the house of the wicked, but He blesses the home of the righteous”.*** Exodus 34:7 speaks of God punishing the children for the sins of their parents to the third and fourth generation. However, this passage also emphasizes God's mercy and steadfast love. While consequences may extend to subsequent generations, God's grace and redemption are available to all who turn to Him.

Both curses and blessings are usually expressed in words. Either spoken or written words. But such words are charged with supernatural power. They are not just ordinary words. And that power that charges them could either be the power of God or the power of Satan. One of the features of curses and blessings is that they continue from generation to generation so that the person who is experiencing them may not even be able to easily discern where they come from—because they may be stemming in the past bloodline generations—even hundreds or years. The good news is that "Christ redeemed us from the curse of the law by becoming a curse for us, for it is written: "Cursed is everyone who is hung on a pole" (Galatians 3:13).

Aspects that make a curse stand effective

Five aspects are very important and significant in effecting any form of a curse. Without these aspects no curse can stand effective. These are;

1. The words pronounced
2. The people involved—both the curser and the cursed.
3. The reason for cursing
4. The place in which a curse is invoked
5. The intended punishments / after effects

All the above aspects are reflected in details in the whole content of this book.

1. The Words Pronounced

The words pronounced play a very big role in effecting any form of a curse. These could be silent or loud, verbal, written or thought. There is a powerful connection between words and cursing. Every word pronounced or thought of in cursing is very powerful. And it [word] is the one that charges the negative and evil energies to make harmful things happen in the life of the one who is being cursed. The holy scriptures in the Bible also warn us about the use of word. Verse twenty one of chapter eighteen in the book of Proverbs warns that;

> ***"…death and life are in the power of the tongue; those who make it a friend shall eat its fruit"[Proverbs 18:21]***
> In the Good News Bible version, the same verse is stated as "***what you say can preserve life or destroy it…***"

2. The People Involved

The people or person involved in the pronouncement of any form of a curse matter a lot in terms of making the curse come into effect. In other words, the magnitude of the effect or punishment or harm caused by a curse largely depends on the person who pronounces it and his/her relationship with the one to whom the curse is being pronounced. For example, people with relational authority over others such as parents and teachers have a great potential of pronouncing a disastrous curse to their children and students respectively. A parent's curse is very effective on his/her children and can cause great harm to them as compared to the harm it can cause to children who do not belong to him/her biologically.

3. The Reason for Cursing

The reasons for cursing somebody determine whether the curse invoked on him/her will stand effective or not. In some instances, if the reason for cursing somebody is not well grounded, say for example, if the person is innocent of the reason he/she is being accused of, then that curse may not come into effect—though this is not always the case. In most cases a curse stands and gets into effect in the life of the person who is being cursed irrespective of whether he/she is innocent or not. A curse can harm anybody. Oppressive forces by evil spirits can bind your life and harm your destiny when others curse you—even when you are innocent. Some people are famously known for cursing others. In some places, they can even be hired and paid to offer the service of cursing. One time I was astonished when I went to one country to conduct a healing and deliverance prayer service and after the service, I was shown an elderly woman whom they said was a renowned professional curser. They said that she could be hired by the people in her locality and paid some money to execute the duty of cursing others. Anyone who had a potential enemy could hire her to curse that enemy

When I spoke to her she admitted that she was involved in that filthy evil practice since she was a young adult. She showed me the materials which she often used in the act of invoking a curse. These included a stick of about one meter long and a small short chair on which she could sit or squat while pronouncing a curse. She also had in possession some other fetish materials which we destroyed with prayer and burnt to ashes. She explained to me a detailed story of the process of how she used to pronounce the curses and the effects those curses caused on the people whom she cursed. She repented and gave her life to Jesus on that day. The final judgement of the fate of her evil acts is between her and the almighty God. It's only God alone who knows what to do with her. As a result of that behaviour, many people feared and often distanced themselves away from her for fearing of picking up a curse from her. Because of this public seclusion she usually lived a miserable lonely life. Even her own children were afraid of her. Only Jesus could redeem her.

4. The place in which a curse is invoked

The place in which the curse is being invoked also determines the severity of its effect. The effect of a curse which is pronounced and invoked in an ordinary house is different from the effect of the curse which is pronounced and invoked in a satanic or occult shrine. The effect of the curse invoked in a satanic shrine is much severe than the one invoked primarily in an ordinary house. This is because the demons and evil spirits in the satanic shrine pick up the curse quickly and re-enforces its effect in the spiritual real. In general, every place can be a standing ground for invoking a curse against somebody or against a nation. However, there are some particular places which evil people use as legal grounds to invoke a disastrous curse against others. These places include satanic / occult shrines, secret lodges meeting places, sea, sea shores or demonic beaches, lakes, grave yards and cemeteries, specific hills or mountains, demonic forests, anthills and many others. The choice of the place in which a curse is invoked depends on the evil intentions of a curser. It is largely believed that the magnitude of the effectiveness of a curse is superimposed by the place in which the curse is being invoked. Some places are known for imposing a curse on whoever gets in contact with them. Because of this reality, some people fear to get in contact with some places for fear of picking up a curse. However, some of such fears are out of sheer superstitions.

5. The Intended Punishments / After Effects

The intended punishment is also another vital aspect in effecting a curse. Each curse that is being invoked on someone or a nation has its own intended purpose and punishment for which it is being invoked. The effect and the harm caused by a curse on somebody largely depend on the intended purpose of the curser. Not all curses invoked yield to similar and uniform punishments. The harm caused varies from curse to curse depending on the primary intention of the curser. However, the effect of all curses is essentially the same—and that is destruction of the human person.

Who Can Curse?

Every human person can pronounce a curse that can cause harm or injury to others. However, there are three major categories of people who are, in a very special way, supernaturally charged with the power to curse. These include:

i) People with relational authority over others

Such as parents, teachers and people in high positions of leadership such as presidents, mayors etc.. Parents are enormously endowed with the power that can curse their children in very many ways.

ii) Men and women representing Satan

Like witchdoctors, sorcerers, occultists, satanists, devil worshippers, obeah men and women, voodoolists, men and women who are members of secret lodges/fraternities etc...

iii) Ministers of faith / men and women representing God

These include priests, bishops, reverends, pastors, patriarchs, popes, cardinals, evangelists, prophets, preachers etc. *A priest may curse someone for violating God's laws. In general, the same people with the authority to bless also have the authority to curse"* (www.thoughtco.com).

iv) God Himself

Disobeying God and acting centrally to His word automatically attracts a curse on humanity. In the scriptures, the bible records some accounts in which God is portrayed as pronouncing a curse. Bible verses like Genesis 3:14, Genesis 3:17, Genesis 5:29, Deuteronomy 28:18 , Genesis 8:21, Genesis 12:3, Proverbs 3:33, Isaiah 24:6 , Matthew 25:41, Malachi 4:6, Romans 9:3, Hebrews 6:8 and others portray a curse resulting from disobeying God. However, God's primary and ultimate wish for humanity is blessings. He always wants us to savour His blessings. God does not impose any curse on human beings but human beings freely throw themselves in the pangs and jaws of the wrath of a curse which God attached on disobedience when they freely choose to do evil. By disobeying God, we are indirectly attracting a curse for ourselves. In other words, when we follow an evil path we indirectly follow a curse.

Deuteronomy 11:26-29 makes it clear that the blessings and curses are already set before us. We are mandated to make a choice from those two. It is our responsibility to choose blessings by obeying God's statues and doing good. Failure to do that throws us on the side of a curse. The scripture contends:

> ***26 See, I am setting before you today a blessing***
> ***and a curse— 27 the blessing if you obey the***
> ***commands of the LORD your God that I am***
> ***giving you today; 28 the curse if you disobey the***
> ***commands of the LORD your God and turn from***
> ***the way that I command you today by following***

***other gods which you have not known...* [Deut.11:26-29]**

Blessings

A blessing is a good fortune from God. It is supernatural. It is not just a wishful thought. It is not just kind sentiment. It is something that is supernaturally empowered to determine someone's destiny and the destiny of his/her descendants. Genesis 22: 16-18 gives an account in which Abraham was willing to offer his son Isaac to God as a sacrifice but God gave him a lamb as a substitute. This is how it is stated:

> ***"...I swear by myself, declares the LORD, that because you have done this and have not withheld your son, your only son, I will surely bless you and make your descendants as numerous as the stars in the sky and as the sand on the seashore. Your descendants will take possession of the cities of their enemies, and through your offspring all nations on earth will be blessed, because you have obeyed me."*** *Genesis 22:16-20*

Because of the obedience of Abraham in God's word, we notice in the above scripture that the blessing was to go through his son Isaac then to Isaac's children and to all his future generations. The obedience of Abraham opened up a door of blessings to all his future bloodline descendants. When we obey God's word and follow His statutes, His abundant blessings gradually start flowing not only in our lives but also in the lives of our future bloodline descendants even if they are not yet born. Obeying God's word and observing His statutes is an act of opening for ourselves and our future descendants an account of blessings. It is the best gift we can give not only to ourselves and our children but also to all those who will come after us.

Irrevocability of a Blessing

A blessing from God is irrevocable. No human being can revoke a blessing that comes from God. In Genesis chapters 25 to chapter 32, we are presented with an account of Isaac blessing Jacob instead of his favourite son Esau. Isaac was blind and prayed for God's blessing to descend upon Jacob. That blessing was meant to be for Esau. When Isaac later realised that he had prayed and invoked a blessing to a wrong person he could not revoke it because he knew that it was not from him but from God. His response was ***"...indeed he will be blessed"*** **(Genesis**

27:33). Scripture records that Isaac trembled violently after realising that the blessing had been given to someone to whom it was not intended. Isaac had regrets in his heart but he could not do anything to revoke the blessing because God's blessing is irrevocable.

> **Isaac trembled violently and said, "Who was it, then, that hunted game and brought it to me? I ate it just before you came and I blessed him--and indeed he will be blessed!"** Genesis 27:33

Once you are blessed by God, no one can take away that blessing from you. It can be obscured by the evil one but never can it be removed completely away from you. This is something we all need to note. A curse can obscure and jeopardize with your God-given blessing but it will never eliminate it completely. Because of this divine reality, your blessing will always flourish again once the curse that had shadowed it is broken and removed. On the contrary, a curse is revocable once there is repentance and forgiveness. Therefore, a curse is something that should not worry us as believers. In Jesus Christ we have victory over any form of curse.

Is a Curse Real?

Many people doubt whether the concept of a curse is something real or not. From the theological and biblical point of views a curse is something real. Take for example in Deuteronomy 27:11-26, God could not allow the Israelites to enter into the Promised Land without being exposed to the knowledge of both blessings and curses if they obey or disobey His commandments.

The tribes of Simeon, Levi, Judah, Issachar, Joseph and Benjamin were selected in a special way to stand on Mount Gerizim when the blessing is being pronounced on the people while the tribes of Reuben, Gad, Asher, Zebulun, Dan and Naphtali were chosen to stand on Mount Ebal while the curse is being pronounced on the people for disobeying God's statutes.

According to this scripture, all people of Israel were mandated to pronounce the word amen on every curse that is pronounced upon them as a way of acceptance that let the curse happen in their lives due to disobedience to God's commandments. In this scripture and indeed throughout the whole bible, the concept of a curse is strongly emphasised not only in the Old Testament but also in the New Testament. Below is how the book of Deuteronomy 27:11-26 records a number of curses:

11 Then Moses said to the people of Israel, 12 "After you
have crossed the Jordan, the following tribes are to
stand on Mount Gerizim when the blessings are
pronounced on the people: Simeon, Levi, Judah,
Issachar, Joseph, and Benjamin. 13 And the following
tribes will stand on Mount Ebal when the curses are
pronounced: Reuben, Gad, Asher, Zebulun, Dan, and
Naphtali. 14 The Levites will speak these words in a loud
voice:

15 "'God's curse on anyone who makes an idol of stone, wood, or metal and secretly worships it; the LORD hates idolatry.' "And all the people will answer, 'Amen!'

16 "'God's curse on anyone who dishonours his father or mother.' "And all the people will answer, 'Amen!'

17 "'God's curse on anyone who moves a neighbours' property line.' "And all the people will answer, 'Amen!'

18 "'God's curse on anyone who leads a blind person in the wrong direction.' "And all the people will answer, 'Amen!'

19 "'God's curse on anyone who deprives foreigners, orphans, and widows of their rights.' "And all the people will answer, 'Amen!'

[20] "'God's curse on anyone who disgraces his father by having intercourse with any of his father's wives.' "And all the people will answer, 'Amen!'

[21] "'God's curse on anyone who has sexual relations with an animal.' "And all the people will answer, 'Amen!'

[22] "'God's curse on anyone who has intercourse with his sister or half-sister.' "And all the people will answer, 'Amen!'

[23] "'God's curse on anyone who has intercourse with his mother-in-law.' "And all the people will answer, 'Amen!'

[24] "'God's curse on anyone who secretly commits murder.' "And all the people will answer, 'Amen!'

[25] "'God's curse on anyone who accepts money to murder an innocent person.' "And all the people will answer, 'Amen!'

[26] "'God's curse on anyone who does not obey all of God's laws and teachings.' Deuteronomy 27:11-26.

Sources of a Curse

There are many sources of curses. Not all of them are exhaustively discussed in this book. However, a substantial number of them are being elaborated. Let us first of all look at the curse in relation to the calling of Abraham in Genesis 12:1-3. This is where God called Abraham when he was still called Abram. There are seven important aspects to note in this particular call.

> ***The LORD had said to Abram, "Go from your country, your people and your father's household to the land I will show you. "I will make you into a great nation, and I will bless you; I will make your name great, and you will be a blessing. I will bless those who bless you, and whoever curses you I will curse; and all peoples on earth will be blessed through you."*** Genesis 12:1-3

When God called Abram, He gave him seven great promises which I may well refer to as the seven great destinies of Abraham's calling. As indicated in the above scripture, these seven great destinies are:

1. I will make you into a great nation
2. I will bless you
3. I will make your name great

4. You will be a blessing
5. I will bless those who bless you
6. I will curse whoever curses you. And lastly
7. All peoples on earth will be blessed through you.

These are real blessings. However, as we can notice, the sixth one is a curse on everyone that curses Abraham. ***"I will bless those who bless you, and whoever curses you I will curse"***.

Many times, God Himself has pronounced a curse on individuals and on nations. A curse is one of God's severest judgements. A curse is part of the package that God promises. In other words, where there is a blessing from God there is a curse too. A curse is always attached to a blessing. That is a very important point for all of us to note. When you curse someone you automatically attract a curse for yourself from God. There are curses which are invoked simply to wish someone ill will—like cursing a neighbour in an argument. That is not good. Always focus on blessing others. When you bless someone, you get blessed too by God. On the contrary, you bind your own life when you curse others.

Causes of a Curse

If there is a curse, there is always a cause for it. A curse cannot exist without a cause for its existence. In other words, a curse without a cause cannot stand. And if a curse is to be effectively broken and removed, its cause must be discovered and dealt with accordingly through prayer, repentance, renouncement, forgiveness and reconciliation. A number of curses are listed in Deuteronomy 27:11-26. From this list, some sources can be synthesised and identified. These include:

1. Dishonouring One's Parents.

Dishonouring one's parents is a serious cause of a curse in one's entire life. The curse that comes because of dishonouring parents is very severe. There are many people I have personally met, who are under severe oppression of the curse of dishonouring their father or mother. Many have problems in their lives because their attitude to their parents is not right. Remember the first commandment was a blessing that God vested in the act of honouring the parents. **"Honour your father and mother that all may be well with you..." (Exodus 20:12)**. In my experience over the past few years I have been actively engaged in the ministry of healing and deliverance, I have never seen someone who dishonours his/her father or mother and life is well with him/her. Such people always have difficulty in attaining a serious breakthrough even though they may pray fervently and even do serious fasting. There are many people out there who are undergoing serious suffering as a result of dishonouring their parents. Dishonouring your parents automatically exposes you to a parental curse that is very hard to break unless there is repentance, forgiveness and reconciliation. Parents need to be honoured at all times of their life. This is because God vested in them abundant parental blessings which are very vital for accompanying and determining the destiny of their children. However, honouring your parents does not mean that you have to agree with them on everything or do whatever they tell you to do but you have to internally and externally honour them as your parents. That is the first perquisite for attracting God's blessing. A parent is the 'earthly god' of any human person.

I know of a young lady in Trinidad who conceived after reconciling with her mother. It happened that this young lady was living with her boyfriend. Her mother never liked her boyfriend and she often ordered her not to get married to that boyfriend. The young lady ignored her mother's order and married the young man whom she believed was her best choice. Together with her boyfriend, they organised their own wedding without the knowledge and consent of her mother. They wedded on the beach into a common (civil) law marriage. Her mother never attended her wedding. When her mother heard of this news she was vexed and very angry with her. Out of disappointment and charged with great anger, the mother shouted at her with many negative words of which ***"you will never have any child with that man and will never have peace"*** stood out the most.

Incidentally, these words turned into a parental curse that haunted her for eight solid years.

Indeed, the eight years this lady lived with her husband were hell. They experienced troubles after troubles. She never conceived in spite of their willingness and readiness to have a baby. Of course, they tried many medical means, but all ended in vein. After attending a few of the healing and deliverance prayer services that usually conducted at the Holy Trinity Catholic Church in Arouca, she got convinced without any reasonable doubt that she was under the oppression of a parental curse invoked by her mother. After many years of not talking to each other, she started making attempts to reconcile with her mother. The initial attempts were futile as her mother had maintained a hard unforgiving heart—hard as a grinding stone. Lucky enough at some point she accepted to reconcile with her daughter.

I was invited by her daughter to lead them in prayer and facilitate the reconciliation process. When I reached their home, the daughter went in and sat on the couch right of their living room. Her mother sat on the other one, opposite of her. At that moment I realised that a tense, sombre mood reigned for about a full minute or two—with both mother and daughter face to face like two disputing hills separated by a river, silent and questioning each other in the inaudible language of their postures and countenances. After a while, the daughter cleared her throat and spoke, tersely looking directly at her mother for the first time since we had entered. She explained the motive of our gathering. After talking for a while anger arose in both and they started 'spitting venom of words' at each other—with each blaming the other of being a 'bad thing'. A fierce fight would have broken out had not the daughter's step father arrived and intervened in the right time. After some moments of calmness, the mother openly confessed how she was unhappy with the choice of a man her daughter had made. In the tribal wisdom of the Baganda people of Uganda (Africa), a tribe in which I was born, raised, and in that respect I belong; there is a saying that ***when an elder does a dance there are aspects of it which the eyes of the young ones cannot see.*** It is also said that ***what an elder sees while sitting on the floor, the young one may not see it even when he/she climbs on the top of a tree.*** Again it is said that ***he who makes one travel through the night wins one's praise in the morning.***

Basing myself on this rich African traditional wisdom, in my personal analysis, considering the fact that she is the only daughter the mother had, the mother always wished her to get married to a man worth of a name. One with whom she can build a home which is rich in traditional wisdom, a home with roots. Not a marriage like the jokes of marriages you often see in the towns and their spineless weddings, expensive and colourful for nothing. Useless marriages which stand their ground like a dry pole and not like a green living tree that gives life to living organisms. Marriages where love knows no courage, patience, tolerance and reverence. As soon as financial challenges, troubles and lack of anything strikes through the door, the love flies away through the window. That was the mother's foresight. On the contrary, the daughter wanted a man who had assimilated much of the modern life, elegant and sophisticated.

After airing out their grievances against each other, they both burst into tears and cried bitterly. They hugged each other and continued crying. They held each other tight for almost 20 to 30 minutes. At the end of it all they both looked into each other's face and said to each other that: ***"I forgive you".*** They had reconciled. At that moment I led them in the prayer of breaking the curse and I asked the mother to pronounce the words of blessings upon her daughter. She invoked blessings upon her and we ended our prayer sessions.

A few weeks later, both shared with me of how peaceful they were feeling after the day of reconciliation. Many things changed for the better in their lives. The young lady conceived. By the time I met her again she was five months pregnant. She is the one I mention about in the introduction of this book. With forgiveness, repentance and reconciliation with her mother she was able to conceive. A parental curse is dangerous. It is the grave of anyone that seeks to give it accommodation. It can bind you. It can hold you and prevent you from conceiving. If you are a person with ears that can hear and eyes that can see, stay away from anything that smells of a parental curse.

A Letter from a deceased mother to her son 3 days after her burial

Note: This is a fiction letter, but it can help us to draw and learn some important lessons concerning honouring parents. Please read it and learn something from it. The original author of this fiction letter is unknown.

***A Letter from a Deceased Mother to her son 3 days after her burial: ***

Dear Son,

I want to know why I died like a poor woman when I have a Son like you. My Son, I wanted to bless you before I die, but now I have gone with my blessings. My breakfast, my lunch and my dinner were one of my challenges when I was alive, but u spent money to cook all types of foods, meats and different types of drinks on my burial day. My Son, you chose to spread and rubbed my dead body with costly fragrance when I was using groundnut oil as my favourite cream. You dressed my corpse with an expensive cloth when it was difficult to buy a wrapper for me. When my corpse was in the mortuary you came to check on me from time to time, you care about my corpse than when I was alive why? The most painful thing is the kind of expensive coffin you put my corpse when I was living in an uncompleted house. When you were young, I starved for you to eat and get satisfied, I wore one cloth in order to provide enough clothes for you. I thought you would take care of me when I grow old. You completed the house, painted it and cleared the compound in one week just to celebrate my corpse. Now you wrote tribute to me saying "Mama, I love you so much rest in peace" - When I died with a broken heart. Finally, my son, I wrote this to remind you that there is no other person that loves a child like a mother. May God forgive you.

2. Idol Worship/Idolatry which we mostly refer to as occult.

This is the primary source and cause of any given curse. Idol worship manifests itself in various ways and practices depending on the religious disposition of the people, their culture and their social, political, economic life as well as their technological advancement. All human societies and nations have forms of idol worship though they differ from society to society. These may take forms like voodoo, obeah, necromancy, witchcraft, sorcery, some forms of new age etc... This is the primary cause of curses in people's lives. The worship of false gods. And according to Exodus 20:3-5, a curse befalls anyone who involves in occult and this curse goes on through the third and fourth generation. You could be suffering from something that was passed on into your life through your great grandparents or their ancestors. In Puerto Rico, for example, as elsewhere in the Afro-Latin diaspora, there is a practice of brujería which draws from indigenous beliefs, African diasporic religions (such as Santería), and European magical practices. This fusion creates a rich but ambiguous multifaceted magical tapestry.

There are many other forms of idolatry today. Money, status, fame, power and even some human beings have become idols for many people to worship as their gods. In Jeremiah 17:5-6 a curse is pronounced on those who put their trust in such idols. In his own words Jeremiah reports:

> ***5 Thus says the LORD, "Cursed is the man who trusts in mankind. And makes flesh his strength, and whose heart turns away from the LORD.***
>
> ***6"For he will be like a bush in the desert, and will not see when prosperity comes, but will live in stony wastes in the wilderness. A land of salt without inhabitant. 7"Blessed is the man who trusts in the***

LORD, and whose trust is the LORD. 8"For he will be like a tree planted by the water, that extends its roots by a stream. And will not fear when the heat comes. But its leaves will be green, and it will not be anxious in a year of drought. Nor cease to yield fruit.

Jeremiah 17:5-8

If you rely solely on your human ability and material resources around you, your own intelligence, your own energy, your own money, your own flesh without honouring God, you may not be far from attracting yourself a curse.

Still in the bible, Prophet Zechariah saw a curse in form of a flying scroll entering into the land and houses of people (Zechariah 5:1-4). Zechariah is hereby narrating his personal experience of encountering the curse. He says-

I looked again, and there before me was a flying scroll. He asked me, "What do you see?" I answered, "I see a flying scroll, twenty cubits long and ten cubits wide." And he said to me, "This is the curse that is going out over the whole land; for according to what it says on one side, every thief will be banished, and according to what it says on the other, everyone who swears falsely will be banished. The

LORD Almighty declares, 'I will send it out, and it will enter the house of the thief and the house of anyone who swears falsely by my name. It will remain in that house and destroy it completely, both its timbers and its stones". Zechariah 5: 1-4

From the above scriptural text, what Zechariah saw in the Old Testament times is not different from what is happening today in our own time. Many families are broken today due to some form of a curse that entered in there. A curse is real and affects the lives of individuals, families, communities and nations. This is because "like a fluttering sparrow or a darting swallow, an undeserved curse does not come to rest" (Proverbs 26:2).

3. Ministers of Faith / Men and Women Representing God.

Ministers of faith are another source of a curse. Part of the ministry of men and women of God such as priests, deacons, reverends, pastors, bishops etc... is to bless people. But they have got also the power to curse. In Joshua 6: 26, Joshua pronounced a curse on anyone who dares to rebuild the evil city of Jericho that the people of Israel had miraculously destroyed and conquered by the power of God. In the New Testament Mark

11: 12ff, Jesus cursed a fig tree and it dried up. The power that the ministers of faith have to bless and curse is really amazing. In Uganda, there is a certain mango tree in a church compound in Masaka diocese. Legend has it that, that tree used to bear many mango fruits season after season. One day the children came to Church and instead of entering into the church to participate in Mass that was going on, they went straight to that mango tree and started eating the ripe mangos. They did not attend mass. When a priest came out after the mass had ended he pronounced a curse on that mango tree that it will never bear any sweet mango fruits since its fruits attracted the children and made them miss participating in the mass. This incidence happened way back in 1970s but up to till today, that mango tree has never bore any fruits. Ministers of faith and religious leaders have got a tremendous power to curse. Therefore, it is advisable for them to use their tongue carefully because it can bless as well as curse.

4. Injustice to the Weak and the Helpless

Any form of injustice inflicted on those at the margins of society attracts a curse on those who perpetuates it. Each person deserves his/her rightful due. Anybody that deprives anyone his/her rightful due attracts for him/herself a curse (Deuteronomy

27:19). Social oppression, political, economic and many other forms of oppression attract a curse to the perpetrators.

5. Parents and People with Relational Authority:

Parents and people with relational authority are another source of a curse. God has ordered human society that one person has got authority over another person or persons. The most obvious example is a father who according to the ordering of God has authority over his family. It doesn't matter whether society agrees to this or not. The fact remains that a father has authority over his family. Second to the blessing of God, the most desirable thing in life is a fathers blessing. And one of the things to be feared most is a father's curse. Many fathers have put a curse on their children either knowingly or unknowingly. It is very common that whenever a child does something wrong, parents especially fathers pronounce comments like ***'you will never succeed in life', 'you are a failure', 'I will never be pleased with you', 'you are good for nothing', 'why don't you be like others, you can never do anything good' etc..*** Sometimes such comments are pronounced in an emotional state or joking manner but they exert a serious curse on the children. It is frightening to see the number of people suffering in life as a result of a parental curse. During my ministry, I have encountered uncountable number of people whose lives are in a mess as a result of a curse put upon them by their own parents. If you are a parent be careful of the words you pronounce on your children because your words can either bless them or curse them. Even if your children do wrong to you, forgive them and refrain from pronouncing at them cursing words. Remember that ***your own child is like an axe, it may fall off your shoulders and cut your flesh open but you still pick it up and hang it on your shoulder again.*** Your child will always remain your child, your own blood, your own DNA no matter what he/she does.

A husband too has authority over his wife. You are free to counter argue this statement but the truth remains that God ordered it in that manner that a husband has authority over his wife. However, this does not mean guaranteeing permission to husbands to abuse their wives under the pretext of exercising their God given authority. A husband is mandated to respect and protect his wife. Because of this divine authority a husband is capable of pronouncing a dangerous curse on his wife. In the same respect a husband is capable of pronouncing a blessing upon his wife. It all depends on how he exercises his God given power. In the bible Jacob pronounced a curse on his wife Rachel which made her die during child birth (Genesis 31:32). She died because Jacob had pronounced a fatal destiny against her. Husbands—respect your wives and support them in a loving relationship. Refrain from cursing them no matter what they do to you. Remember the famous saying that what goes round comes back round. When you curse others the same curse comes back to you. And when you bless others, the same blessings come back to you.

6. Teachers

Another kind of person that can curse is a teacher. A teacher's curse can haunt his/her students because a teacher has got authority over them. It is possible that a teacher may have a personality clash with a student and he/she pronounces a curse on the student that ***'you will never learn, you will never succeed, you will never get through, you are a stupid child*** etc...' It is advisable for teachers to always refrain from using such words against their students because such words may turn into a curse that may haunt those students for the rest of their entire life.

Anybody in any position of authority has got power to curse all those under his/her jurisdiction. For example, a president can pronounce a curse on a nation and that curse can affect the entire nation. A top most manager or director can impose a curse on the entire institution or organisation. A mayor can pronounce a curse that can affect individuals in his/her area of jurisdiction.

Women too as life givers have the power to curse. Being life givers through giving birth, women have got a special power to curse or bless humanity. For example, the tears that a woman may shade under painful moments such as rape, child neglect by the husband, sexual abuse, assault etc... can impose a curse on whomever brings such painful experiences in that woman.

7. Self-Imposed Curse.

This is another commonest curse. Many people impose on themselves a curse without knowing or without intending to do so. Very often people pronounce curses on themselves through the words they say about themselves. They can say for example that ***I cannot succeed, what is the good of living, what is the purpose of living, nothing good is in me, I wish I can die, I'm bored to death*** etc... This is like imposing a spirit of death on yourself. Very often such statements (negative confessions) are made during the peak of desperation. These are terribly dangerous statements to utter because they determine one's destiny. A typical example of a self-imposed curse is found in the sin of trying Jesus by Pontius Pilate as recorded by Mathew 27: 24-25

> ***When Pilate saw that it was no use to go on, but that a riot might break out, he took some water, washed***

his hands in front of the crowd, and said, "I am not responsible for the death of this man! This is your doing!" And all the people answered, "let His blood be on us and on our children!" (Mathew 27:24-25)

From this scripture, it can be noticed that the people imposed on themselves a curse that would affect not only themselves but also their future descendants. This is a typical example of a self-imposed curse that prevails from generation to generation. In some cases, we suffer the consequences of a self-imposed curse by our ancestors. The history of the Jewish people cannot be separated from this self-imposed curse even up to today. Many people attribute the crisis, wars and turmoil which have been happening in Israel for centuries to this curse which their ancestors imposed on their nation. A self-imposed curse is very serious. Be careful with what you say and pronounce on yourself because this determines your destiny. Always use positive words of affirmation or positive confessions to yourself and your future generations. Use words like ***'I'm blessed', 'I am a winner', 'I will succeed', 'I will have everything in abundance', 'evil has no power over me' etc....***

<u>8.</u>Illicit and Deviate Sexual Practices.

This is another serious cause for a curse in one's life. Any form of deviate sexual practices brings a curse on those who practices it. Sexual intercourse with people of the same gender, sexual relations with an animal, incest, sex with children, rape, defilement, sex with multiple partners, sex with people who are involved in occult, sex with father or mother-in-law, sex with step father or step mother, sexual intercourse with own mother or father all bring a curse to those who indulge themselves in it.

<u>9.</u>Mixing Prayers with Anti-Christian Practices.

Another sullied source of a curse is mixing prayers with anti-Christian practices. Some people lack sufficient faith in the power of Christian prayers. Due to this lack of faith, they mix Christian prayers with spiritual services from other sources which are not Christian as a backup. I have known a number of Christians who go to church for prayers and at the same time go to seek spiritual services from witchdoctors, sorcerers, obeah man/woman, secret lodges and fraternities like free mansions and Iluminati, witch-hunters, witch-finders, santeria etc...

Others seek services from some people who claim not to belong to any religion but are spiritual and therefore they refer to themselves as 'spiritual guides'. Such people present themselves as 'God's agents' anointed by God Himself to offer spiritual services to people. They offer prayers and supplications and very often perform rituals of some spiritual significance. Some of these so called 'spiritual guides' are agents of satan and so whatever they do is purely satanic, evil and profane. They normally mix the sacred with the profane and truth with falsehood and in the end the ordinary person cannot tell which is which. I was one time told a story by a woman in Arouca-Trinidad who was formerly working as a 'spiritual guide' in one of the 'spiritual centres' in Trinidad but quit the service after a serious break-up with her fellow 'spiritual guide' not only over money issues but also after feeling guilty conscience.

She said that before quitting her job as a spiritual guide, she and her fellow 'spiritual guides' usually went to Mt. Saint Benedict—a famous Catholic monastery belonging to the Order of Benedictines. This monastery accommodates a number of Benedictine monks—both priests and brothers of which majority are advanced in age. Regular Masses, prayers, retreats and other spiritual services are being conducted in this monastery on a daily basis. She told me that they usually went there and collected holy oils, incense, holy water, blessed salt and blessed candles from the monks. After collecting these items from the monks, they could take them to the obeah man (witchdoctor) and mix them with their concoctions, waters, salt, incense and other items from the obeah man. The obeah man could perform some rituals and invocations on such items and make some sacrifices on them in order to make them 'fit' for use. After that, these 'spiritual guides' could distribute these items to their clients of course at a very expensive fee. When clients go to these people due to desperation, they cannot tell whether the items are profane or not. This attracts a curse.

Mixing prayers with anti-Christian practices or mixing sacramentals with anti-Christian rituals attracts a curse. It is something very dangerous that you must do everything possible to avoid. It is equivalent to stripping your mother naked and doing terrible things on her. Some people cannot acquire total deliverance and breakthrough due to the fact that they are involved in this evil practice. If you are a person with ears that can hear and eyes that can see, stay away from anything that smells of mixing prayers with anti-Christian practices. This is the grave of anyone that dares to give it a chance.

I have a friend who lives in San Raphael (a place located in eastern part of Trinidad). I was one time chatting with her via WhatsApp text messages. Through these WhatsApp text messages she shared with me of her experience of mixing prayers with other anti-Christian practices. I revisited these messages which she corresponded with me on the 17th of August 2018 and made a synthesis that I compiled. This is what she texted to me:

> *"Well from my experience I visited a "Spiritual Mother". That was her title in the...********...Church [name of the church concealed] So I would say that is another name given to obeah man or woman. She gave me 'baths' with funny smelling oils for protection, prosperity, breaking spells, etc. Her group also carries you to the sea if the need arises. But they don't refer to themselves as obeah people. They refer to themselves as men and women of God with great gifts. Many of them advertise their services from all over in the miscellaneous section of any newspaper. They state the wide range of things they guarantee e.g bringing back lost lovers, winning court cases, giving wealth and prosperity etc. A normal bath with the oils and bushes can start from lowest Trinidad and Tobago dollars 1,000 because the oils are expensive. Going to the sea to rid you of curses, etc....will require another person to help him or her to flip you and stuff so it can start from TT $5,000- $10,000*
>
> *A friend of mine....who is a teacher went to this Spiritual Mother for help. The Spiritual Mother gave her a reading about her problems. She told her that her daughter would*

die in 3 days' time but to save her life.. ..they would have to bathe her by the sea and bury her body in the seashore sand and do a ritual to save her life. They charged her TT $10,000. She did not do it. And her daughter did not die in 3 days' time as she had claimed.

They also come to your home upon request to perform baths and rituals for protection. The mopping of your home with turpentine, red lavender, etc... are commonly used in this country. Also the placing of square camphor at the doorways in your home and corners are commonly practiced by the same Christians. People think it is another form of help from God when they visit these places and take spiritual advice from these people. I can say this because I was one of those persons.

I remember I went to Mount St Benedict one day sometime last year...and I was relaxing in the seating area outside when a mature couple started chatting with me and then asked me if I wanted help with any situation, I can go to Auzonville Mall in Tunapuna....where "oils" are sold by a woman there. Oils such as "money oil" to rub in your business place etc... to get customers and to solve various other problems are sold for TT $100.

They implied that the holy oil from the mount is bought by these spiritual people and are mixed with their own concoctions and resold for a higher price and with the claim that it solves problems.

Reiki Healing is another popular thing people engage in. I'm not sure but I saw my niece interested in doing it. She brags about channelling your "energy" and the element of the universe and all sorts of crap. I have a friend from school who does it as well. But I don't know if she is still into it.

These practices we think are ok or the practices we feel will 'help God' or 'speed up' breakthroughs. But most of the time it is a short-cut because people only want what God has to offer but developing a relationship with Him is not in their plans.
Many people go back and mix other prayers given to them and they are not aware that what they are doing is wrong".

[Name concealed on owner's request]

Avoid mixing Christian prayers with prayers from other sources claiming that it is also from God. Every time you go to get your palm read or go to get wealth and prosperity charms for yourself or your family you are attracting a curse for yourself and your entire bloodline. With each visit you make to these places you are derailing your original destiny which God has for you. That is why if you heed to these practices your life goes back in the same cycles. Have total trust in Jesus, develop a personal relationship with Him and the prayers will work for you. There is absolutely nothing else you can do to 'speed up' the effectiveness of prayers except developing a serious personal relationship with Jesus. All the rest you can do are vanity or vanities which does nothing except ruining your life.

10. Secret Lodges/Fraternities/Societies and Covenants with Evil People:

Secret lodges are another source of curses. In Exodus 23:32. God warned the Israelites about the people whose nation they were about to enter. They were all wicked and an idolatrous nation. This is what God said to Israel **"Do not make a covenant with them or with their gods".** From this scripture, it is clear to us that if you make a covenant—which is a solemn agreement with evil people who are under the power of evil forces you too, come under the power of those evil forces.

All over the world, there are secret societies/fraternities and lodges who are characterised by mysterious rituals and hidden agendas. The commonest and widely pronounced are *The*

Illuminati, Skull and Bones, Freemasonry etc... These are just a few examples of such. Secret lodges are sure roads for disasters to you and your future descendants. I can't estimate the number of crippled, retarded and unhappy men and women, children and adults whose current problems go back to a parent or grandparent or great grandparent in Freemasonry. The consequences of engaging in such lodges are ordered by God and are disastrous. The Catholic Church considers Freemasonry, for example, incompatible with its teachings. Active participation in Freemasonry is forbidden for Catholics due to the fundamental conflict between Catholic doctrine and Masonic principles

<u>11.</u> Men and Women Representing Satan.

Men and women representing Satan are a terrible source of curses. They include witchdoctors, sorcerers, occultists, Satanists, devil worshippers, obeah men and women, voodoo practitioners, witch hunters, witch finders, those who do necromancy etc... In every human society there are such people irrespective of race, colour, ethnicity, nationality etc... The name given to such people and the way they carry out their evil activities varies from place to place depending on the culture and technological advancement in which they operate but the purpose of what they do is essentially the same everywhere. Such people are experts at cursing and their curse produces terrible outcomes. That is their speciality and they are very skilful in cursing. They know exactly when and how to curse. I have personally met many people in different countries who are tormented by curses from these witchdoctors, magicians and satanic agents.

When I was in Trinidad and Tobago—a country located in the Caribbean, a certain woman who looked to be in her late fifties or early sixties came to me privately asking for prayers. She was experiencing a sharp pain in her vagina [you may call it her private part if you wish]. According to her the pain had lasted for more than two decades. No medicine could cure her. She spent so much on moving from hospital to hospital and meeting different medical experts in addition to carrying out her personal search for remedy on the internet. In spite of all these efforts, she never got cured and medical doctors could not diagnosis exactly what was wrong with her. When she was narrating to me her story, I realised that a curse had been placed upon her by a malicious person who was envious of her success. That malicious person consulted an obeah man (witchdoctor) who placed a curse on her never to be well in life. Because of this curse she lost her marriage, her husband was snatched away from her, she became barren and failed to conceive and many other unfortunate situations befell her. All the pain she was experiencing was a result of this curse. I did not reveal this to her but I took her in the prayers of breaking the curse. I also gave her the prayers to be praying for a certain period of time. I did not pray for her healing but I prayed for the breaking of the curse that was the source of her problem. This woman came back to me two weeks later testifying to me that she was healed completely of her vaginal hurts and pains. In a short time she was healed of the problem that had lasted for over 20 years and the medical science had failed to provide a solution. It is always necessary to diagnose the real source of the problem and then discern how to handle it. Today she is a free woman. She has no pain. And there is not much we did except breaking the curse upon her. Curses are real. But in Jesus Christ we have victory over all curses. If you don't know what you are dealing with then you always remain a looser. Today we are so much technologically secularised that we don't believe in these spiritual realities yet they are very real and affect humanity even if we don't acknowledge their existence and influence.

12. Negative Utterances, Bad Wishes and Negative Prayers:

These are another source of a curse. James chapter three, verses fourteen and fifteen speak of them as *"wisdom which does not come from heaven"*. He says:

> ***[14]But if you harbour bitter envy and selfish ambition in your hearts, do not boast about it or deny the truth. [15]Such "wisdom" does not come down from heaven but is earthly, unspiritual, demonic.*** *[James 3:14-15]*

In this scripture James talks about two kinds of wisdom. The first kind is that **one which is not God's wisdom**. According to him this kind of wisdom has three characteristics. And these are:

i. It is earthly
ii. It is unspiritual and lastly
iii. It is demonic

There are some people whose utterances and prayers are not authentic at all. This is because sometimes they pray with bitterness, envy, revengeful thoughts or self-seeking ambitions. Such utterances and prayers don't yield blessings instead yields negative energies that tantamount to curses. Or sometimes in our Christian communities, believers speak evil against one another, run one another down, criticise one another etc... This generates negative power against the individual victims. Sometimes such negative power comes from the people who are quite close to you. I have seen some men and women who have been sick and bed-ridden for years simply because their wives or husbands have had a death wish for them.

I met a man in Chaguanas-Trinidad who was bed-ridden for years. Medics could not establish exactly what he was suffering from. This man was suffering as a result of a curse from his wife whom he had unlawfully divorced. The woman held a death wish for him since the time of divorce. This death wish became an evil spell that released a negative power that haunted him for years. Most strikingly, the woman just uttered that "because of the emotional pain and trauma you have caused to me, I wish you can die". This wish was charged by demonic forces. That statement "I wish you can die" haunted this man in real sense. He was constantly on the verge of death. He spent much of his resources in pursuit of his medical treatment which never registered any successful relief. It's after we prayed the prayers of breaking the curse that he was freed and got better.

There are a lot of things in the human soul that we cannot fully understand by our earthly wisdom. The human soul has got a lot of power that can do good or evil. If it is under the control of the Holy Spirit, it can do good but if the soul is under the control of other evil spirits, it can be so powerful to enforce evil.

13. Murder

Murder is a serious cause of a curse. Anyone who commits murder or assists in executing murder or accepts money to murder an innocent person commits a grave offence that brings forth a dangerous curse on both him/herself and his/her future bloodline descendants. Through experience in the ministry of healing and deliverance, I have known a number of people who were under bondage and oppression of this curse. Deuteronomy 27:24-25 warns about this kind of curse.

The Relationship Between Curses and Blessings

Both curses and blessings are words that are charged with supernatural power. They are words which impose on people's lives good or bad fortune and to a large extent determine their destiny. A curse is the opposite of a blessing: www.thoughtco.com stresses that:

> ***"Whereas a blessing is a pronouncement of good fortune because one is initiated into God's plans, a curse is a pronouncement of ill fortune because one opposes God's plans. God may curse a person or a whole nation because of their opposition to God's will. A priest may curse someone for violating God's laws. In general, the same people with the authority to bless also have the authority to curse."***

The Basic Cause and Source of Curses and Blessings

Chapter twenty-eight of the book of Deuteronomy gives a full account of blessings and curses. In these verses, the sources of blessings and curses are clearly listed. The basic source of the blessings is obedience to the word of God. You don't need to chase blessings from God. What you actually need is to meet the conditions for receiving blessings and then God's blessings will come your way. And the cause of curses is disobedience to the word of God. I encourage you to read this chapter in order to acquire a detailed understanding of this basic source of curses and blessings.

Signs and Manifestation of God's Blessings in One's Life

Blessings and curses manifest in different ways in different individuals, communities and nations. All people are blessed by God. If they obey God's statutes, His blessings may manifest themselves in their lives in the following ways.

1) Strong faith and belief in God.
2) Possession of admirable qualities especially if such qualities run through most of the family members. Such qualities include but not limited to: intelligence, great wisdom, great leadership skills, beauty, academic and intellectual brilliancy, financial success, cheerfulness, fortitude, success in marriage and relationships etc...
3) All time exultation i.e being lifted up.
4) Good health
5) Creativity and re-productiveness i.e reproducing and bearing fruits in every area of your life. Whatever you lay hands on succeeds and multiply, if it is business, it incurs great profits.
6) Success and victory in many aspects of life
7) God's abundant favour

8) Joy, peace and happiness even amidst moments of trials and suffering.
9) Your presence being a hope for many.
10) Being loved by all.
11) Most of your plans follow through even in unexpected circumstances

Signs and manifestations of a curse in one's life

1. Failure to serve the Lord God the way you would wish to.
2. Constant frustrations
3. Something holding you back every time you try to succeed
4. Fighting something you don't fully understand.
5. Rampant suicides and unnatural deaths in a family
6. Constant humiliation
7. Any time you are on the verge to succeed something happens and you fall back.
8. Chronic accidents over and over again
9. Failure to reproduce in any area of your life. Whatever you lay hands on does not succeed.
10. Finding it hard to have a breakthrough
11. Chronic family breakdowns

12. Continuing financial insufficiency even when your salary is good.

13. Frequent mental break down and mental disorders in the family especially generation after generation.

14. Frequent emotional breakdown and mood swings

15. Repeated miscarriages and related female problems especially if they run through most family members.

16. Repeated or chronic sicknesses especially without clear medical diagnosis.

17. Some forms of abject poverty

18. Lack of favour.

19. Constant rejections

20. Always broke even when you are working

21. No Job promotion or salary increase even with the required qualifications and experiences.

22. Failure to get a gainful job even when all the conditions for getting it are in your favour. However, not every case of lack of a job is due to a curse. A careful discernment is necessary here.

Note that: some of the above signs may be due to other factors but about 80 percent of them point to a curse.

Other warning signs that your life could be under a curse

Below is a proposed general checklist that can act as a guide to help you do thorough self-examination leading to self-discovery. It will help you discover whether there is an underlying curse prevailing in your life or not. If you have or are experiencing multiple signs and symptoms from the checklist, then you are most likely under the influence of a curse and therefore urgently need deliverance. Find out whether:

- You were involved with the occult, witchcraft or voodoo.
- Whether you are attracted to, or have consulted palm readers, satanic advisors, diviners, witchdoctors, obeah men or women.
- Whether you have ever involved yourself in White occult magic.
- Whether you have an addiction to gambling.
- Whether you were involved in secret organized lodges and groups such as freemasonry, illuminati, skull and bones etc...
- Whether you feel like there is a force pushing you to do wrong things against your will.
- Whether you have a history of rebellious behaviors in your life or in your family.
- Whether your parents contemplated aborting you.

- Whether you feel deep or severe personality changes like fear or wanting to be isolated all the time.
- Whether you have suicidal thoughts and tendencies.
- Whether you have toxic unexplained bodily odours and foul smells like that of a dead body or corpse or burning sulphur. Even if you use strong deodorants, the smell remains.
- Whether you often hear voices or thoughts in your head that are negative, persuasive, or commanding you to do something evil.
- Whether you have been chronically ill all your life without proper medical diagnosis.
- Whether you have panic attacks or phobias on a regular basis.
- Whether you experience tremendous hostility or fear when encountering someone involved in deliverance ministry.
- Whether you have been consistently prone to accidents all your life.
- Whether you have a history of sexual perversion in your bloodline (adultery, rape, incest, etc.)
- Whether you feel something chocking and suffocating you from time to time.
- Whether you have engaged in a lifestyle of cheating, robbing, theft and murder.
- Whether you are extremely uncomfortable around people.

- Whether you have fits of anger or rage that are unusual for you.
- Whether you are intensely jealous of others.
- Whether you have had an abortion.
- Whether you have sudden unexplainable anxiety that cripples you.
- Whether you have chronic headaches or mental confusion.
- Whether you get headaches or feel uncomfortable anytime you look at religious objects such as Bible, Cross, Rosary etc.
- Whether you feel uncomfortable socializing or spending time with church people or people who pray fervently.
- Whether you feel that in a certain area for example your house, there is something heavy, depressive or oppressive.
- Whether you feel controlled by a power contrary to your will.
- Whether you feel some unnatural movements in parts of your body.
- Whether you encounter chain problems and life trials which do not end.
- Whether you have feelings of being under attack or threatened when others don't.
- Whether you have horrible experiences in your dreams especially seeing snakes biting you.
- Whether you have emotional disturbances.
- Whether you suffer from restlessness.

- Whether you experience persistent miscarriages without proper medical explanations.
- Whether you were once involved in Satanism and devil worship and its related activities.
- Whether you are constantly harassed by evil spirits
- Whether you suddenly get creepy or scary feelings.
- Whether you have addictions to drugs
- Whether you have usually had sudden depression.
- Whether you have hatred and bitterness toward others for no justifiable reason.
- Whether you have feeling of hopelessness.
- Whether you have an evil trend of problems in your family.
- Whether you were involved in sexual promiscuous behaviors such as prostitution.
- Whether you have strange beings engaging you into sex especially at night.

Take a careful note that if you have just one or two of the above symptoms it could be caused by other factors and not necessarily a sign of a curse or demonic control in your life. Some psychiatric and medical deficiencies can cause similar conditions. It is therefore extremely recommended that you first consult your doctor to make sure there aren't any physical or serious mental or emotional issues that need medical or psychiatric attention.

However, if your answer is yes to most of the above, then you need spiritual deliverance. It is important to immediately start praying against them. In your prayer ask God to deliver and heal you. You can write them on paper if you want and then pray against each of them one by one. If such signs persist, you may need the spiritual services of a minister of deliverance or an exorcist.

Effects of a curse on somebody's life.

A curse may no longer be still present in somebody's life but its consequences may still continue to linger in one's life. Such consequences may continue to gravely damage the person's life and personality until such a person receives inner healing. Therefore, in some cases praying the prayers for breaking curses may not be sufficient enough to bring a complete wellness in a person. Such prayers may need to be accompanied by the prayers for inner healing. A combination of the prayers for breaking curses and inner healing brings about a superb recovery for anybody under the oppression of any unexplainable realities related to a curse. The consequences of any given curse may affect the person in many but not limited to the following ways:

1. Chronic anxieties

2. Depression
3. Lack of progress
4. Failure in everything that one does
5. Constant suicidal thoughts
6. A conviction that you are not able
7. Hearing of strange and abnormal voices
8. Seeing of strange and abnormal visions
9. Making the person useless even when he / she is well educated and well disposed.
10. Constant partnership with wrong people.
11. Fear to try even what you can
12. Inferiority complex
13. Feeling of hopelessness
14. Persistent bad luck.
15. Persistent streak of unfortunate events
16. Persistent nightmares

How to set yourself free from a curse

The very important thing to note is that the power to break any given curse in your life is within you. You have got the power to break any curse. Power is not in a priest, in a bishop, in a brother, in a pastor, in a sister or in any other prayerful person that you may think of, but power is in you. Make good use of it. Use if profitably for your own benefit.

The first step to break any form of curse is to understand that the provision and price to break any prevailing curse was already paid by Jesus Christ on the cross at Calvary. If you read Galatians 3:13-14, you will discover that Jesus Christ already paid the price which we were meant to pay for our iniquities. Scripture recons that:

> [13] ***Christ has rescued us from the curse pronounced by the law. When he was hung on the cross, he took upon himself the curse for our wrongdoing. For it is written in the Scriptures, "Cursed is everyone who is hung on a tree."*** [14] ***Through Christ Jesus, God has blessed the Gentiles*** *[none Jews]* ***with the same blessing he promised to Abraham, so that we who are believers might receive the promised Holy Spirit through faith.*** Galatians 3:13-14

Take note of the exchange as indicated in the above scripture: the death of Jesus on the cross was atonement for our deserved eternal punishment. In Jesus Christ we have victory over any form of a curse.

He bled and died that we may have life; he was bruised and wounded that we might be healed (Isaiah 53:5-8). He was made sin that we might be made righteous (2 Corinthians 5:21). He was rejected that we might be accepted (Isaiah 53:3-12). And finally, he was made a curse that we might enter into a blessing (Galatians 3:13-14). This is the basis of God's redemption for human kind.

The curse is so real. God wouldn't have made Jesus a curse if it was not something real. God made Him (Jesus) a curse so that through Him we may be delivered. Jesus became a substitute so that we can be made a blessing because he was made a curse. God is not stupid that He can make us be delivered from something that does not exist.

All deliverances have to be made in faith of what Jesus did for us on the cross at Calvary. Through the death of Jesus, a blessing is already legally ours. What we need now is to move from the legal basis to a practical one. We have to make this blessing get working in our lives.

Steps to follow in the breaking of a curse

1. First of all we need to ascertain the real cause of the problem in our lives. This is not always easy. However, in many cases through prayers and the working of the Holy Spirit God reveals to us the sources of the curse that might be haunting us. In many cases God wants us to know what

we are being delivered from. If God reveals this to you don't deny it but instead recognise your problem and its cause, repent of a thing that led you into that curse, renounce the curse and resist repeating the same.

2. Confess your faith in Jesus Christ because he is the high priest of our confession and it is through him, with him and in him that we can have victory over any curse.
3. Confess any known sin of yourself and of your ancestors especially that which lingers in your family
4. Commit yourself to obedience in Christ and his word.
5. Forgive others especially those in your family whom you believe are the source of the curse. Even if they are dead. Still forgive them.
6. Renounce all contact in secret lodges e.g. Freemasonry, Illuminati.
7. Get rid of the contact objects which are connected to idolatry e.g. images, Ouija boards, Jewry, mystical stones, sticks, rings, oils etc...
8. Release yourself and rebuke every curse in the name of Jesus because you have the power to do that. Scripture tells us that whatever we bound on earth shall be bound in heaven and whatever we lose on earth shall be loosed in heaven (Mathew 8:8).

In summery, breaking any curses involves the following

- **Awareness:** Recognizing patterns and acknowledging their roots.
- **Repentance:** Turning away from sinful behaviors and seeking God's forgiveness.
- **Renewal:** Embracing God's truth, healing, and transformation.
- **Prayer and Intercession:** Praying for deliverance and freedom from generational patterns.
- **Claiming Christ's Victory:** Jesus' sacrifice on the cross breaks the power of sin and curses (Galatians 3:13-14).

Then pray the following prayer regularly. At least pray it consecutively for the first three weeks.

A Prayer for breaking every curse

Pray this prayer regularly but most importantly at least pray it consecutively every day for the first three weeks. This prayer contains two parts namely:

Part One and Part Two. It is advisable that you pray both parts all at once and conclude them with a prayer of self-dedication to Jesus as written below. However, for the interest of time, if you don't have enough time to pray both parts, just pray only part one in the morning and then pray part two in the evening/night before you sleep. If you choose to pray each part separately, still don't forget to pray the prayer of self-dedication to Jesus at the end of each part. The prayer of self-dedication to Jesus should accompany both parts. If you have enough time then pray both parts at once.

Part one

You can pray this part in the morning: Conclude it with the prayer of self-dedication to Jesus

In the name of the Father and of the Son and of the Holy Spirit: Amen. Lord Jesus Christ, I believe that you are the son of God and the way to God the Father, I believe that you died on the cross to take away my sins and rose again from the dead to give me eternal life. I renounce all my sins and I return to you Jesus for mercy and forgiveness. I renounce pride, rebellion, disobedience, stubbornness and self-centredness. I humble myself and come to you as a little child and ask for forgiveness and deliverance.

In order to receive your blessings and be freed from any curse, I first of all confess my sins and the sins of my ancestors..... ***[here mention all your known sins that you remember to have committed....you can mention them silently (or loudly if you wish).....]***

Lord I thank you and I believe that you have forgiven me all the sins I have mentioned. I also forgive myself and forgive others who hurt me. **[*Here mention the names of all those who hurt you...*],** I forgive all these people and whoever else that harmed and wronged me.

Vengeance belongs to you God, not me. I forgive everyone who has hurt me and pray for their souls because they don't know what they have done to me. In Jesus' name, I transfer all pain, betrayal, rejection, abuse, trauma, shame, guilt and abandonment to the cross of Jesus Christ. I let go of all anger, resentment, hatred, thoughts of revenge and every malicious thought I have been having in my heart. Father in heaven as, I forgive them, please forgive me too and give me the grace to totally forgive them from the bottom of my heart.

In the name of Jesus Christ, I break and loose myself and my family from all curses caused by habits, charms, hexes, spells, jinxes, satanic powers, sorcery, witchcraft, soul ties, negative utterances, evil wishes, violence, trauma, physical bondages, death wishes, mental bondages, incest, illegitimacy, abandonment, rejection, divination, necromancy, voodoo, Santería, brujeria, and obeah, on my family, both mother and father's side going all the way back to the first parents.

I break and loose myself and my family from any vows I made and those made by my ancestors; from any person or any occult or psychic sources, and any demons coming through the bloodlines. I cancel all invitations and dedications made to evil spirits. Father in heaven, I break and renounce all evil soul ties that I have ever had with (lodges, fraternities, sexual partners, close friends, relatives, engagements, cults, occult objects, drugs, gambling, porn etc...). I renounce all these ties and declare them destroyed in the name of Jesus.

I renounce, break and loose myself from all demonic subjection to my parents or any human being, living or dead, who has dominated me in any way against the will of God. I ask you to remove any kind of occult objects in my house that honour Satan and dishonour Jesus. And every evil influence. I thank you Jesus that on the cross you were made a curse that I may be redeemed and blessed. Because of that which you did to me, I release myself now from any curse that has been keeping in bondage.

In Jesus' name I destroy every weapon formed by Satan to attack my life, and I refuse every tongue that is raised to accuse, oppress and curse me in any way. I command satan, to loose the finances of people who owe us money, and all the things you have stolen from my family that are lawfully belonging to us through the blessings of Jesus. Father, please send your angels to bring these things back to us. I pray all these trusting in the powerful and unfailing name of Jesus Christ our Lord. Amen.

Part Two

You can pray this part in the evening/night before you sleep.

Conclude it with the prayer of self-dedication to Jesus

Merciful and ever loving God, I firmly proclaim that Jesus Christ redeemed me from the curse of the law by becoming a curse for me, for it is written: "Cursed is everyone who is hung on a tree" (Galatians 3:13). In the name of the Lord Jesus Christ, I now bring the fullness of his cross, death, blood, and sacrifice, his resurrection, life, and empty tomb, his authority, rule, and dominion; I bring judgment from the Lord Jesus Christ against every Satanic force, foul power, witchcraft, magic, hexes, evil spells, voodoo, obeah, strong man, evil eye and curse. I bring Jesus Christ cursed for me against all curses that have been raised against me—written, spoken, unspoken, or transferred to me.

[If you know what the exact curses are, it helps to name them. For example, you may say... all curses of death,...all

curses on my marriage,...all curses on my health,...all curses on my finances... etc...etc...]

I bring the precious blood sacrifice of Jesus Christ, the Son of God, whose blood was shed upon the cross, against all blood sacrifices and rituals and their every claim against me. I bring Jesus Christ, the Son of God, sacrificed for me, against all ritual sacrifices and their every claim against me.

I bring the dedication of Jesus Christ for me in death upon the cross against all ritual dedications. In the name and by the blood of Jesus Christ, I break the power and hold of every curse that has come to me through ritual or ritual sacrifice.

In the name and by the blood of Jesus Christ, I break the power and hold of every curse that has come to me through transfer by another human being. In the name and by the blood of Jesus Christ, I break the power and hold of every curse that has come to me through words spoken. In the name and by the blood of Jesus Christ, I break the power and hold of every curse that has come to me through occult practices.

In the name of Jesus Christ, I command all demonic spirits that have gained access to me through curses and rituals cut off and banished from me and my household, in the mighty name of the Lord Jesus Christ. Jesus, I ask you to send your angels now to completely disarm all curses, hexes, evil spells, voodoo, magic and obeah from me; disarm their every device and render them destroyed. I ask your angels to remove all foul spirits involved in these curses and bind them to your feet for judgment.

In the name of Jesus Christ, I declare every legal hold and every legal ground of the enemy Lucifer broken, disarmed, and destroyed. Satan has no hold over me now through curses or occult practices, through sacrifices or any ritual of any kind. Through the blood of Jesus Christ, I am free. I am set free from any curse and demonic bondage. Thank you Jesus, for setting me free. I order these curses and claims utterly disarmed and dismantled now, through the power of the blood of Jesus Christ, and in his name.

I now claim every spiritual blessing that my Heavenly Father has given to me in Christ Jesus as according to Ephesians 1:3. [***here mention the blessings you are claiming from God. For example you may say....I now claim for the blessing of good health, blessing of good marriage, blessing of finances....etc...etc...]***

I claim those blessings and many others which I have not mentioned but God destined them for me. I claim them to come to me right now, by the authority and power of the Lord Jesus Christ, and in his name. Jesus, may these things be fully accomplished now through your mighty name. I give you thanks and honour and praise. All of this I pray by the authority and in the mighty name of our Lord Jesus Christ of Nazareth Amen.

Now conclude with the prayer of self-dedication to Jesus below

Prayer of Self Dedication to Jesus

Lord Jesus Christ, through your precious blood which you shed at Calvary, I am redeemed out of the hand of the devil, all curses are wiped away and all my sins are forgiven. The blood of Jesus Christ, cleanses me from all sins. I am justified and made righteous, just as if I had never sinned. I am set apart for God. My body is a temple for the Holy Spirit, redeemed and cleansed by the blood of Jesus. I belong to Jesus now, body, soul and spirit. His blood protects me against all evil. Satan has no more power over me, no more place inside of me. Curses have no more power over me. I renounce all evil spirits completely and declare them to be my enemies. Jesus said: "And these signs shall follow them that believe: In my name shall they cast out devils: …." (Mark 16:17). I am a believer, and in the name of Jesus Christ, I exercise my authority and expel all evil spirits. I command them to leave, according to the Word of

God and in the name of Jesus. I dedicate my entire life to Jesus Christ. And from now onwards I re-affirm that I belong to Jesus Christ and that He is my Lord and saviour. Amen

Take Note of this : Trust in God

Keep doing self-deliverance by praying every day and submitting your will to God. This may take weeks or even months. Keep going. Don't lose heart. At times you may seem as if you are going nowhere. Remain focused even in those moments when you feel low and disappointed. Give those disappointments to Jesus. Deliverance is a gradual process. Be patient and hopeful in Jesus Christ at all times. At the end of it all you will emerge victorious.

Testimonies

Throughout my pastoral activities, I have journeyed with different people in different life-threatening situations; –through prayer, counselling and spiritual direction, God has done amazing miracles for them. Each week I receive volumes of testimonies from people testifying to the great wonders God has done in their lives. After a careful research, examination and follow-up, undisputable authenticity was found in them and so I requested those people to put them in writing. Below I introduce them to you in their own words.

Evil spirits used to harass me at night.

My name is Simona [not her real name]. I come from eastern Trinidad. I would describe the past fifteen (15) years of my life as very uncomfortable for the most part. Our home had fights between my mother and father and a lot of arguments with my mother and either one of us. My father had no voice. My eldest brother who is mentally ill would get "sick' often in a violent way and had to be forcefully taken to St Anns Hospital [commonly known as the mad house] quite frequently. We would share jokes as a family at times but it was short lived. Our home had six people: My mother, father, three (3) brothers and me. My sister is married and lives her own life.

My mother kicked me out of our home to live with my then boyfriend when I was twenty three (23) years old. The relationship lasted less than 2 years so I had to return home. Things did not change much. It got worse. It was very hostile. My mother insisted that we do our own cooking and maintaining of ourselves. We ended up, with a house with six people, four (4) fridges, four (4) stoves. Everyone had their own groceries, wares, washing detergent, cleaning supplies, etc. It was a general understanding that every man was for himself.

Just to reflect, my dreams indicating witchcraft activities started around the age of fifteen (15). The dream was always the same: I was in our bedroom (the one my mother and I shared) and there

I would stand cleaning her wardrobe with a broom or I may be cob webbing the room or dusting it out. This dream kept recurring several times ever so often for sixteen (16) whole years. I am now thirty-one (31) years old. I did not understand it. I talked to close friends from church about it but they were puzzled as well.

It was very difficult to pray. I had problems sleeping because of the fights at night and the television being on late deliberately. But more so, I also had problems sleeping because evil spirits would harass me at night. I was poked and pulled about my body, molested sexually, saw and heard things that were not real. I would cry and be frustrated but I would not stop praying.

It was October 0f 2016 that a representative from the Catholic Education Board of Management (CEBM) came to our school for a one day visit when they introduced the staff to a Novena called 'Mary Undoer of Knots'. Instead of doing the Novena for the recommended nine (9) days, I restarted at the end consecutively for about two (2) months! What drove me to this? Desperation. Even though I had a great job as a teacher and had a car, I was not happy. My mother was treating me badly with insults and accusations. I was tired of this humiliating life. My life was going nowhere. My living arrangements were uncomfortable. Even though I was working, I was always broke. No man stayed with me in relationships for long. They enjoyed the sex for a while and left.

However, I was not prepared for what happened next. One night in mid December of 2016, I got a dream about being in my mother's bedroom again. I was sweeping the room in my dream as usual when suddenly I pushed the broom below her bed and what I pulled out with the broom was so shocking, it woke me from my sleep, only to fall asleep almost immediately to re-dream it in the exact way: There was this book with a hard cover covered in dust. In the dream I sensed the book was a 'Bad Book' with prayers that was not of God.

That was all the confirmation I needed. A fire stirred within me. God chose to show me the root of my problem which appeared to stem from my mother.

I made a decision on Christmas Day after my father and mother almost fought to the death that morning because she refused to make a Christmas Day meal. I was not living like this anymore.

I confided in a friend and I regretted taking her advice. I sought the help of a Spiritual Guide who told me that my mother was practicing witchcraft and that my life was under a curse. I paid him some money to offer me a few ***'Bush Baths'*** *that were meant to break the curse and bring prosperity into my life. It did not work out. In spite of the fact that I underwent a bush bath, nothing changed in my life. I continued to live a miserable life.*

I found an apartment in .... and moved in it on December 31st, 2016. The few people who I told that I moved out and it was motivated by a dream, thought that I was over- reacting and crazy to uproot my life on a 'perhaps'.

I can remember the month of January 2017 and early February with feelings of despair that my God took me out of the only place I knew as home where I referred to as 'Egypt' because it reminded me of bondage and placed me here in .... to rent in an apartment unsure if I would make it on my own. I was of the notion that once I moved out from home, my problems would go away. I was wrong. Even though my past experiences had decreased a bit, I still had sleeping problems, saw and heard things and was still poked and prodded at night. I was frustrated that I did not have a boyfriend like a normal young woman. I cried to God one night so bitterly in mid February that I threw myself on the cold tiled floor and refused to move. I wept and was going to give up.

My tears stopped when I heard a voice as clear as day say, "Simona, you have to go on a Daniel Fast". I got up and saw no one. I said to myself that it must be the Holy Spirit. I dried my tears and did some research as I was not familiar with that fast. I followed instructions the next day.

It was the longest and most frustrating three (3) weeks; but 21days came to an end. It was unbelievable: in a matter of days, I got a salary increase. The week following that, a letter came to my school addressed to me stating that I got a job promotion that I waited 10 years for. Glory be to God! That was so unexpected! God honoured my prayer and fast. What was impossible in ten (10) years was possible in 21 days.

After discovering the root of my delays in life, I started to earnestly tap into the power of Prayer and Fasting for Breakthroughs. For the next few months that followed, I embarked on a total of (four) 4 Prayer and Fasts during July and August that were for 3- day periods with partial food. The rewards were amazing. God revealed to me in dreams that I was not praying as I should and he taught me how to supercharge what I was already doing by directing me to scriptures, showed me how to use His word, which are Laws. He showed me how to attack altars levied against my life and how to speak with authority to shut down evil operations in the spirit realm. I was obsessed until the final 3 days of a Prayer and Fast ended with some shocking news: I got a call from my brother saying that my mother was diagnosed with Breast Cancer. I started to panic. Did my prayers unknowingly cause her to get ill? We were not on speaking terms but I would never direct my prayers to anyone. I felt afraid and stopped adding fasting to my prayers.

I took care of her from that same August of 2017. During that time I embarked on two, 3- day Fasts and one Daniel Fast for protection as I was around her daily. She admitted to me on her hospital bed that she had not slept in her room for years and it was the couch she slept on. She could not say why. She further added that she used to worship and still worshipped the Sun and the Moon gods and that she would never stop. She would make a sacrifice to get her healing. I tried telling her about Jesus Christ but she would not listen. Oh yes, I also received a ten (10) year salary adjustment arrears that was huge. I thanked God for another breakthrough but my mother was dying. The cancer was already at stage four (4).

In November 2017, I was recommended by a priest to get help from the intercessory prayer group from St Charles RC in Tunapuna and following up with other people of God in 2018 who were able to guide me, they were of help but was still unable to fulfil my requests to come to my mother's house where the wardrobe which was allegedly the altar she had used to perform her rituals, is still to this day there with nobody to help us in the proper removal of it. I found no further help which led me to continue praying for God to provide the answer.

After talking to my mother one more time to persuade her to stop worshipping those false gods, she shouted at me in rage, "I don't want to hear anything. I pray to Jesus and all of them too!" I felt sorry for her. She was obviously mixing Christian prayers with Satanic prayers. A few days later after that conversation, she stopped talking and eating. She started to lose her mind on her hospital bed. She would speak in an unknown language and stopped recognizing familiar faces. She would defecate in her adult pampers and smear the faeces all over her body. She was forced to wear handcuff- like straps on her bed as a result. I was so embarrassed that I asked the nurses to limit visitors. She eventually died on December 29th, 2017 at the age of 70.

I feel passionately about this topic of Self-Imposed Curses as my research into this topic during my months of prayer and fasting stemmed from my experiences of household wickedness that has plagued my life and family bloodline for many generations. From what I have noticed, Self-Imposed Curses and Generational Curses both go hand in hand as they are linked to the same type of sin.

My family have engaged and some are still practicing all types of Idolatry for as far back as four generations and beyond. I was told that my great grandmother was originally from Dominica and her husband from Barbados but they migrated to Trinidad. She was a known Obeah Woman in the area who had " Prayers" and would often speak in the language of Patois. She was feared by many. Her cause of death is unknown as she just completely vanished one day after taking a walk. Some say she was Senile, some say she was taken by the devil. She did however; make an oath stating, "0ne day I will leave and no one will find me". And indeed her body was never found. Even though a relative rebuilt a house on the same spot where her house was, it was haunted by evil spirits and prayers of deliverance was administered by some church members. It is believed that she introduced those evil practices into our family. She had twelve (12) children and almost all of them repeated her rituals in many ways, her children, grandchildren and great grandchildren have followed what they were pre-disposed to do.

Some of them went to the Obeah men/women who used what I now know as Divination/ Retrieving information from the world of Familiar Spirits to furnish them with information: for healing, removal of curses, etc..., and some of them performed the "innocent' rituals themselves in what I now know the title as Witches/Wizards.

My bloodline was/are into: Reading of "Bad Books", Reading of Psalms from the Bible with the intention of causing harm to others, selling their children to the devil in exchange for luck, taking regular baths at home with red lavender, lime and blue soap to get rid of 'blight', hog blood rituals, worshipping the sun and moon to gain the powers to 'see' or 'travel', doing wickedness to people for revenge, saying negative things to one another, obtaining readings from spiritual guides about their current affairs, what the future has in store for them; and yes, even to break curses that were levied against them from neighbours, etc.

Most, if not all the members of my family tree were/ are shockingly Christians and they were of the belief that practicing these rituals were to enhance their quality of life and that of their children as an act of helping out Jesus because he [Jesus] responds too slow to prayers, or was simply an act of unknowingly mixing regular Christian prayers with rituals to enhance the result i.e to get quick results. I myself, as mentioned before, out of ignorance and desperation in December 2016, made paid visits to a Spiritual Guide to break curses in my life but it did not work. I later knew that my actions were setting up my future generation with curses. I of course repented of that.

Unfortunately, this iniquity had harsh effects on some my siblings, uncles, aunts, cousins, etc for generations:

1. *Mental illness in each generation- A total of six (6) persons in my family has been diagnosed.*
2. *Antisocial Behaviour- Those who never went to St Anns Hospital divulged in a lot of antisocial behaviour such as Alcoholism, theft, prostitution, having sex with their own*

biological sons, incest (many cousins in sexual relationships producing offsprings) suicide, drunkenness, etc.

3. *Sickness/Infirmity- Eye problems/ blindness, Cancer, Hypertension, Diabetes, infertility.*

During my journey to deliverance, I discovered a lot of things about the things that keeps us in bondage.

1. *That sin of that nature is what God detests the most above all other sins because it is Idolatry.*

2. *When your sin of that nature becomes a habit and you do not acknowledge it as sin it upgrades to iniquity which makes things worse. That God cannot go back on his word and it is therefore an automatic Generational curse.*
3. *That my prayers for a happy life did not reach God as it should because I was unaware that my bloodline, which was practicing all 0f this caused a stain of iniquity upon the innocent ones like myself and others who were praying earnestly, that G0d cannot act in the messy iniquity I was unknowingly in. I felt cast off for sins i did not even commit.*

4. *What I did not know was that I was praying for the wrong things at the time: house, car, husband, happiness. I did not know that I needed to pray for deliverance first. I also ignored my dreams for several years of the root of my problem and simultaneously was under the bondage of what I now know as household wickedness by my mother. So I was already under the confines of a generational curse and then I later found out that my mother had sacrificed me. Her altar, the wardrobe is still at the house.*

5. *It was after praying and fasting I discovered that it is important to repent of not only your sins but of those of your fore parents, parents, grandparents, siblings, etc, for knowingly or unknowingly practicing witchcraft/ idolatry.*

6. *That when you are seeking God to remove you from that curse, you have to attack in prayer the altars and evil covenants at the root for it to be consumed by the fire Of God and not only the Agents Of the devil. This can only be done by prayer and fasting because of the nature of the iniquity.*

7. *If your life was knowingly or unknowingly dedicated to a curse or you were sacrificed, it takes time to be completely free from that type of bondage. Just because you wake up one morning and decide to give your life to Christ after being in bondage for seventy years does not mean He will deliver you after you decide to seek deliverance after one prayer session.*

I was healed of breast cancer and my daughter got a good job

I am not the type of person who visits the doctor regularly. However in 2017 my GP and I became well acquainted. In January, just after the New Year I developed a severe case of asthma where I lost my voice for 2 weeks. I was prescribed some potent steroids as the usual ventolin inhaler and prednisolone were not working.

In June due to renovation works in the office I had another asthma attack. The doctor then said I would have to take a certain medication every day for the rest of my life to manage the asthma. I am not a fan of pharmaceuticals so I was not sold on the idea. I used the medications for 11/2 months until I felt better. In August my left knee started to hurt. At the end of the healing seminar in August, Brother Stephen Kakande asked all persons with knee pains to come forward and he prayed with us. The next morning the pain was worse, I was baffled. As the week progressed the pain worsened, so again I went to the doctor. She said there was some swelling and inflammation and sent me for an x-ray.

I collected my results on Thursday 7th September 2017, I remember the date because that night I discovered a lump in my left breast. Back to the doctor; the next day with my x-ray results and another problem. She said my body was reacting to stress. Immediately following were mammogram, ultrasound and a biopsy. The results indicated stage 3 ductile carcinoma or breast cancer, meaning there was tumor in the lymph node and one in the left breast.

Up to that point only my children knew what was happening. I decided to deal with this journey ……….

1. Faith

2. Family and friends

3. Food

4. Focus

I then told my parents and my close friends. I asked my friends to come pray with me before I started treatment. I had just completed the "Life In The Spirit Seminar" and Br. Stephen Kakande's Healing of the Family Tree novena, so I felt God had been preparing me for this journey, I was in a prayerful 'state' and felt calm. My children had also observed a few of their father's relatives battle various forms of cancer, many did not survive. So I knew I had to weigh my options carefully and select the most effective treatment.

I was recommended for 8 sessions of dose-dense chemotherapy (every 2 weeks) starting on October 25th 2017 to shrink the tumor. I was blessed to have Dr. Sheppard as my consultant as he was patient and answered any question, explaining the procedure and even giving me a handout about the drugs I would receive and their side effects. My daughter suggested that he should be my doctor, he politely replied that it doesn't work that way but I saw him 60% of the time. God's work.

I was also blessed that there was never a day I went for chemo and drugs were not available, or I had to postpone a session because my blood platelets were too low. I was lifted up in prayer everyday by friends and family.

I adopted a supplement regime with the help of a friend to combat the effects of the chemo and was mindful of my diet. I had eliminated sugar, rice and flour from my diet upon my diagnosis to starve the disease. To be honest the only side effects I suffered were extreme fatigue for 3-4 days after chemo, slight darkening of my palms, joint and muscle pain with the second drug and neuropathy in my hands and feet. And the most obvious, hair loss.

After the 2nd chemo the lump in the lymph node was undetectable. After the 4th session the one in the breast was also undetectable. According to the doctors that was good news and bad news. The lump was seemingly gone but they didn't know where to operate, as the original plan was a lumpectomy. When I had finished chemo in February I was sent for another ultrasound, this too showed nothing. I underwent surgery in March and received the histology in May that confirmed no signs of cancer. Praise be to God.

My daughter graduated from UWI (University of the West Indies) just after my 1st chemo treatment and was my chauffeur and constant support throughout this journey. My son would administer the injections I took home, 6 injections after each session. My daughter saw all her friends getting jobs and was worried about her prospects and didn't want a job she would not enjoy. I assured her that the Lord had seen how much of a support she was to me that He would bless her with a job she wanted when the time was right. Two (2) days after I was told I was cancer free my daughter was call for an interview. She scored highest in the interview and got the job she wanted. Praise be to God.

Two weeks before the doctor cleared me to return to work I got the offer of a promotion. I accepted.
We never know what the future holds but God does. Three years ago when the Bethesda community was asking for volunteers, I suggested to my children that we should join, especially as my son has a gift of working well with children, they respond positively to him. Little did I know that one of the members would become an important supporter in my cancer journey, as she had begun her journey in 2016. Her support, generosity and compassion have been invaluable. Again I believe God led us to Bethesda.

Although I am cancer free now, I am not cured. I pray every day with an attitude of gratitude and I ask God to sustain my strength and resilience to maintain the lifestyle I need. He's not done with me yet.

Cherryann D.
Arouca-Trinidad.

Sources

Scanlan Michael and Randall J. Cirner. Deliverance From Evil Spirits.

A Weapon for Spiritual Warfare. Servant Books, Michigan, 1980.

https://www.merriam-webster.com/dictionary/curse

https://www.thoughtco.com/what-is-a-curse-248646

https://www.bing.com/search?q=what+is+a+curse&form=EDGHPT&qs=DA&cvid=10e406593dd0417a8520bd98886a4520&cc=GB&setlang=en-US&PC=LCTS

Other books authored by Fr. Stephen Kakande C.S.Sp

Stephen Kakande C.S.Sp has authored several books since he was a seminarian. His publications are highly regarded for their outstanding role in transforming the lives of many people around the world. They are written in different languages and include:

Those translated into Spanish

1. 10 maneras para hacerte crecer fuerte en la fe
2. 40 días de liberación--Oraciones para desbloquear sus bendiciones dadas por Dios
3. Cómo Orar Y Recibir Ayuda De los Santos Ángeles
4. Como Interceder por la Victoria Personal en Momentos de Prueba

Those in English include:

1. Crossing From Slavery To Freedom
2. 10 Ways To Make You Grow Strong In Faith
3. 220 Dreams and Their Interpretation Plus Prayer Solutions for Each Dream.
4. 40 Days Deliverance Novena Prayer To Unlock Your God Given Blessings.
5. 9 Ways To Tap God's Blessings.
6. 15 Days With Jesus
7. 1000 Dreams and Their Interpretation Plus Solution Prayers for Each Dream-Book 1.

8. 1000 Dreams and Their Interpretation Plus Solution Prayers for Each Dream-Book 2.

9. 1000 Dreams and Their Interpretation Plus Solution Prayers for Each Dream-Book 3

10. Pray Your Way To Effective Deliverance

11. How To Break That Curse

12. How To Do Deliverance

13. How To Pray And Receive Help From Holy Angels

14. How to Intercede for Personal Victory in Trials.

15. Stations of the Holy Spirit—A Pilgrim's Prayer Manual.

Those in Luganda include:

1. Novena Ey'enaku 40 Eyokusumulula Ebisibye Emikisa Gyo.
2. Ebirooto 250 Amakulu G'abyo N'essaala Ezigendera ku Buli Kirooto.
3. Engeri Yokusaba Nofuna Obuyambi Okuva Mu Bamalayika

Those in Runyakitara (Runyankole / Rukiga) include;

1. Ebiro 40 By'okushumuururwa Kw'eshaara Za Novena, Okwigurira Emigisha Ei Ruhanga Akuha

Those in Swahili include;

1. Novena ya Siku 40 ya Kufungua Baraka Ulizopewa na Mungu

To access them on Amazon use the following link

www.amazon.com/author/fatherkakandecssp

ABOUT FR. STEPHEN KAKANDE C.S.SP

Fr. Stephen Kakande Sekayala, CSSp. is a priest of the Catholic Church and a member of the Congregation of the Holy Spirit popularly known as The Spiritans or Fathers of the Holy Spirit. He is a Ugandan born in Kampala (Africa). He studied Philosophy, Religious Studies and Social Sciences at the Queen of the Apostles Philosophy Center (PCJ) – Jinja (Uganda) – a Catholic Missionary Consortium affiliated with the Pontifical Urban University of Rome (Italy) and the University of the Uganda Martyrs (Nkozi), from which he obtained a bachelor's degree. He also holds a degree in Theology from the University of the West Indies (Trinidad and Tobago). She also holds a certificate in Intercultural Studies awarded by the Tamale Institute of Intercultural Studies (ICCCS) in Ghana. He pronounced his first vows on .06.2016 in Lushoto-Magamba in Tanzania, and his final vows on 16.06.2019 in Arouca-Trinidad and Tobago. He was ordained a deacon on 21.06.2019 in Port of Spain, Trinidad and Tobago. He was ordained a priest on 21.11.2020 in Mulago, Kampala, Uganda. He is a renowned preacher and teacher of God's Word, intercessor, pastoral counselor, and author. In addition to serving in his home country of Uganda during his formation period, Stephen has served for some time as a missionary candidate both in Africa and beyond, particularly in the countries of Zambia, Ghana, Zanzibar-Tanzania, and Trinidad and Tobago. He conducts Healing and Deliverance prayers, Intercession, Pastoral Counseling, and direct preaching for Metanoia (life change) on the radio, Catholic charismatic retreats, and popular missions both locally and internationally. His publications are highly regarded for their outstanding role in transforming the lives of many people around the world. He is the founder of the Holy Spirit Prayer Center in Uganda and the Mount Sinai Family Network; a private union of lay men and women of diverse backgrounds, cultures, and nationalities united by a common goal of passionately serving God and the Church through different ministries. Fr. Stephen is a man with many talents, gifts, and a wide range of pastoral concerns. More importantly, he is known as a humble, charming, loving, peaceful, and devoted man. He exercises parish ministry in Puerto Rico (USA)

Made in United States
Orlando, FL
05 November 2026

90231065R00056